DOWN SYNDROME
resources *ra*
and activities

GW01551384

Sentences and grammar checklists and record sheets

Child's name	
Date of Birth		**Sex**	Male / Female
Address	
Date first completed	
First completed by	
Notes	

A publication of The Down Syndrome Educational Trust

DSra-04-01-(en-gb) (January, 2001)

http://www.down-syndrome.info/library/dsra/04/01/

First published: January, 2001

Revision: 1.01

ISBN: 978-1-903806-37-1

A publication of The Down Syndrome Educational Trust

The Sarah Duffen Centre, Belmont Street, Southsea,
Hampshire, PO5 1NA, United Kingdom.

Telephone	+44 (0)23 9285 5330
Facsimile	+44 (0)23 9285 5320
E-mail	enquiries@downsed.org
Web Site	http://www.downsed.org/

The Down Syndrome Educational Trust is a charity, registered in England and Wales (number 1062823).

Proceeds from this publication support future research, services and publications. The production of this book provides employment for adults with Down syndrome.

Concept and design: Frank Buckley.

Typeset, printed and distributed by a wholly-owned subsidiary of The Down Syndrome Educational Trust:

DownsEd Limited
The Sarah Duffen Centre, Belmont Street,
Southsea, Hampshire, PO5 1NA.
United Kingdom.

Sentences and grammar checklist

The checklist should be completed and retained by parents as they will have the most complete knowledge of their child's communication skills. Some parents will welcome the help of a teacher or speech and language therapist as the checklist is also to be used to help to plan language teaching activities. The list is intended to be used as a supplement to the speech and language modules in the *Down Syndrome Issues and Information* series.[DSii-03-01, DSii-03-02, DSii-03-04] The information in these modules should be read before completing this checklist or starting a speech and language programme with your child. This checklist is part of a set of checklists covering all aspects of speech, language and communication skills. In addition to 3 vocabulary checklists there are checklists for interactive communication and play,[DSra-03-01] speech sounds,[DSra-02-01] and sentences and grammar.[DSra-04-01] This checklist should be used in conjunction with the other checklists as all aspects of communication skills should always be considered in parallel.

How to use the sentence and grammar checklist to assist your child to learn to talk

This guide to the way in which sentences and grammar develop should be used in conjunction with the vocabulary checklists. This checklist is different from the vocabulary and speech sound checklists as it is a guide to types of constructions, rather than specific words or sounds. Your child will begin to use sentence constructions with a variety of vocabulary. Your child is learning grammar all the time you are talking to them in natural sentences. You do not need to take a course in analysing English grammar to help your child to learn to use grammar and sentences, but it is helpful to be aware of the early stages of grammar development in order to be able to help your child with games and reading activities.

One simple rule will be effective for teaching sentences and grammar, once your child begins to put two and three words together, and that is:-

Listen to your child's key words and expand them into the shortest complete sentence.

For example: *"Daddy gone"* to *Daddy has gone"*

"Cat sleeping" to *"The cat is sleeping"*

"Play sand" to *"Can I play in the sand, please?"*

"Mummy go car" to *"Mummy has gone out in the car"*

"Daddy go work" to *"Daddy is going to work"*

You will already be using these expansions naturally (without thinking) as you talk to your child during the day at home or at school. This simple approach will also ensure that you teach using examples that are relevant to your child and can be used by them when they want to talk.

You can use the same strategy when thinking about making simple books. Words that you wish to teach from the vocabulary lists, such as prepositions and joining words will also give you ideas for sentences to practice in games or with reading activities. For example *"Put the book on the table"*, *"The shoe is here not over there"*, *"There is a dog and a cat"*, *"If you get your coat, we can go out"*, *"We need our coats because it is raining"*.

We encourage you to make use of an observation diary particularly to help you observe and encourage your child's grammatical development and ability to use longer sentences. Keep a notepad handy and note down the phrases and sentences that your child is using, both in imitation and spontaneously. This will help you to be aware of exactly how he or she is putting words together and it will help you to follow the guidance on expansion above.

The main aim of this checklist is to encourage you to informally assess your child's current grammar comprehension and production and provide you with the opportunity of recording your child's progress, as he or she moves beyond the one word stage of communicating. It will take a child a number of years to master all the grammar discussed in this checklist and he or she will understand the grammar long before using it in spoken language.

Individual rates of progress

There is little published information on the way in which, or rate at which, children with Down syndrome develop grammar and sentences in their spoken language. We know from our practical experience that there are large individual differences. Some children will be using one or two words together at five years of age, others will be using four and five word sentences. Some teenagers will be using complex sentences in their everyday communication but many will still be using 'keyword' sentences, without all the joining words and word endings in place. Since limited verbal short-term memory may be a major factor delaying progress in spoken language, reading activities may be the key to teaching grammar, even for children who are not independent readers and need full support to read. Individual progress with sentence production will be affected by speech difficulties but one way of improving these is also by practising longer sentences, supported by print.

Key word sentences, if the words are intelligible, will be effective for everyday communication, so the amount of time that is put into trying to teach your child to use complete sentences has to be an individual decision. Children's progress and

their enthusiasm for learning will be linked to the improved effectiveness of their language in their everyday lives.

Syntax and Grammar

Syntax refers to understanding the way word order changes meaning, for example, *"Pat hits Mary"* does not mean the same as *"Mary hit Pat"*. Similarly *"Daddy has gone to work"* changes from a statement to a question if we change the word order to *"Has Daddy gone to work?"*

Grammar to refers to the 'bound morphemes', the word endings that change meaning (for example, *'ed'*, *'ing'* or *'s'*) and the 'function' or joining words such as *'a'*, *'the'*, *'is'*, *'are'*, *'if'*. Function words seem to be the most difficult for children with Down syndrome, though this is also true for other children with speech and language impairments.

Building sentences - syntax

The early sentences produced by children are keywords put together - usually nouns, verbs and adjectives - used to express the key points of the message but without the grammar. The word order of the keywords in these sentences is usually correct.

Two words together

At first children use single words to communicate and then they begin to put two words together to convey more information.

Comprehension

When your child understands some 50 words, it is important to play games that demonstrate two ideas and to use the two word phrases as you do so. Ideas for these games to teach comprehension and production of two-word utterances can be found in *Speech and Language Development for Infants with Down Syndrome (0-5 years)*. [DSii-03-02] The list provided gives you examples of the range of different meanings that children express in two-word utterances. It will be useful to play games to model examples of each of them. Your child's use of all the different types of 2 word utterances is an indication of her/his growing understanding of the world and events in it.

Production

When your child has between 50 and 100 spoken words or signs you can expect and encourage him or her to begin to say or sign two word utterances. Within a few months of using two words together, you can encourage your child to use 3 word utterances to extend the ideas that he or she can link together and communicate about. These 2 and 3 word utterances use key words, usually nouns, verbs and adjectives with some prepositions.

There is little detailed research on the emerging sentences of children with Down syndrome at this point. Remember that children will understand two and three keyword combinations before they can say or sign them. Remember also that speech clarity affects the amount of words that children will attempt to link together in a sentence. Your child may hold back from combining more words together if people do not understand when he or she uses longer sentences. It is useful to encourage your child to put signs together to produce longer phrases if they have difficulty with speech production, while at the same time, helping them with speech sound work.

From our practical experience, we are not certain that children with Down syndrome do use all the same 2 word combinations in their speech as typically developing children. However, we do want them to be able to link the same range of ideas together and therefore encourage you to use this list as a guide for activities. However, do not worry if your child makes different combinations or does not say all of the usual ones. If you are interested in helping us gather further information on this, you might like to record your child's 2 and 3 word utterances for us - contact The Down Syndrome Educational Trust and you can be involved in a study of emerging expressive grammar and receive regular advice in return.

Two word stage

Category	Example	Understands	Signs two word utterance in this category	Says two word utterance in this category
Agent - Action	*Mummy push / Baby sleep*	☐ __/__/__	☐ __/__/__	☐ __/__/__
Action - Object	*Drink juice / Throw ball /*	☐ __/__/__	☐ __/__/__	☐ __/__/__
Agent - Object	*Daddy shoe (as he puts shoe on)*	☐ __/__/__	☐ __/__/__	☐ __/__/__
Possessive	*Mummy car / Sally doll*	☐ __/__/__	☐ __/__/__	☐ __/__/__
Descriptive	*Blue ball / Big truck*	☐ __/__/__	☐ __/__/__	☐ __/__/__
Position (place)	*In box / Slide down*	☐ __/__/__	☐ __/__/__	☐ __/__/__

Temporal (time)	Go now / Biscuit later	☐ _/_/_	☐ _/_/_	☐ _/_/_
Quantitative (number)	Two ball / One cup	☐ _/_/_	☐ _/_/_	☐ _/_/_
Conjunctive (and)	Cup plate / Shoe sock	☐ _/_/_	☐ _/_/_	☐ _/_/_
Existence	This bear / That biscuit	☐ _/_/_	☐ _/_/_	☐ _/_/_
Recurrence	More milk / More biscuit	☐ _/_/_	☐ _/_/_	☐ _/_/_
Non-existence (none)	No bear / All gone juice	☐ _/_/_	☐ _/_/_	☐ _/_/_
Rejection (don't want)	No milk / No banana	☐ _/_/_	☐ _/_/_	☐ _/_/_
Denial (this isn't)	No juice / No daddy	☐ _/_/_	☐ _/_/_	☐ _/_/_

Three word stage

It is helpful to model two and three keyword utterances to help your child to extend his or her spoken word combinations, attention and understanding. However, you should talk to your child in ordinary grammatically correct sentences as you do so, stressing and signing the keywords in the sentence. When your child uses two or three keywords in speech or in sign, it is important to respond by expanding and extending their utterance into the shortest grammatically correct sentence. Your child should only be encouraged to model keyword utterances until they can put 3 words together. At this stage it is important to ask them to copy or to read grammatically complete and correct sentences (for example *"Daddy has gone to work"* not *"Daddy gone work"*). There is little research on the emerging grammar of children with Down syndrome and in our experience, it is important to practice correct grammar rather than wait for it to emerge - especially for children of four years and older - for more information on this point see the practical modules

Category	Example	Understands	Signs two word utterance in this category	Says two word utterance in this category
Agent - Action - Object	Dad hit ball / Sally kiss doll	☐ _/_/_	☐ _/_/_	☐ _/_/_
Agent - Action - Locative	Mum go store / baby go bed	☐ _/_/_	☐ _/_/_	☐ _/_/_
Action - Object - Locative	Drink juice kitchen / Take shoe car	☐ _/_/_	☐ _/_/_	☐ _/_/_
Phrases with prepositions	Car in box / Hide under table	☐ _/_/_	☐ _/_/_	☐ _/_/_
Phrases with modifiers	Want more cheese / See my dog	☐ _/_/_	☐ _/_/_	☐ _/_/_
Carrier phrases	I want biscuit / I see plane	☐ _/_/_	☐ _/_/_	☐ _/_/_

These are just some examples and your child will probably use many other three and four word sentences, such as in questions *"Where man go?"*, *"Want eat my snack"*, *"Mummy read 'nother book"* or statements *"Going see Nanna car"*. Note them in your observation diary to guide you when choosing sentences to work on.

Question forms

Your child will display understanding of question such as *"What's that?"*, *"Who is coming?"* from quite early, and they will ask questions at the one and two word stage by pointing - but use of question forms in spoken language will come later. Remember to use them as you talk to your child - and to use *"can"* and *"will"* - *"Can you come here please?"*, *"Could you go and look for your shoes, please?"*, *"Will you take this to dad please?"*, *"Will you drink up your juice please?"* It is possible to model questions and answers to encourage your child, for example you say, *"Why are we putting our coats on? - Because it is raining"* or *"When are we going out? - When Granny comes"*.

In your observation diary, keep a note of the way in which your child 'asks' questions and his or her use of question words. You will also be marking question words such as *"What"*, *"Where"* and *"When"* on the vocabulary lists.

Negatives

As all parents soon find out, from quite early on children understand and use 'no' when they do not want something or they do not want to do something! Children can be helped to understand negatives in a wider range of uses with simple games such as placing objects in a bag, with one odd one out - for example 4 cars and an animal - and saying *"Is it a car?"* as you take each one out - then *"Yes, it is a car"* or *"No, it is not a car, it is a dog"*. Picture materials can also be used to teach negatives, for example *"He has a hat on"*, *"He has no hat on"*, or *"He hasn't got a hat on"*. Games to encourage your child to use negatives can be played - *"Have you got a hat on?"* - and the answer modelled *"No, Billy hasn't got a hat on?"* This game can be played in front of a mirror, with a hat!

In your observation diary, keep a note of the way in which your child indicates negatives and his or her use of 'negative' words. You will also be marking them on the vocabulary lists.

Grammar

When your child has some 250 to 300 words in his or her vocabulary, he or she will begin to use some of the grammatical markers (for example for plurals or tenses) and more of the function words in their sentences, until they talk in grammatically complete sentences. When you begin to work with Vocabulary Checklist 3, you will use these markers on the words used in sentences.

Tenses, plurals, possessives, and the use of is, are

Definition	Example	Date first achieved in spoken language	Example of child's use
The (-ing) ending on verbs	*He's drawing*	☐ __/__/__	_____
The preposition "on"	*Put it on the table*	☐ __/__/__	_____
The preposition "in"	*It's in the cupboard*	☐ __/__/__	_____
The plural /s/	*Dogs bark*	☐ __/__/__	_____
The irregular past tense of verbs	*It broke / He ran away / I made it*	☐ __/__/__	_____
The possessive /s/	*Tom's book*	☐ __/__/__	_____
The uncontractable "be"	*He is / they are (In reply to "Who's there?")*	☐ __/__/__	_____
The articles "a" and "the"	*a dog, the car*	☐ __/__/__	_____
Regular past tense 'ed'	*Sally picked a flower*	☐ __/__/__	_____
The /s/ for singular verbs	*John rides the bike*	☐ __/__/__	_____
The use of "has" and "does"	*He has a car / Mummy does the shopping*	☐ __/__/__	_____
The contractible auxiliary "be"	*He's laughing / Mummy's cooking dinner*	☐ __/__/__	_____

Plurals

The use of /s/ on the end of a word to indicate a plural is a grammatical rule that is learned early in typical development. Simple games can be played to show one or more than one item, using the singular and the plural forms of the words. Children with Down syndrome may understand the plural /s/ but not be able to put the /s/ on the words they say because of speech sound production difficulties.

There are a number of plural words that are irregular such as feet, and teeth. These just have to be learned and some of the most common ones are in the vocabulary checklists.

In your observation diary, keep a note of the way in which your child indicates 'more than one' and the words that he or she is using. You may be marking some of them on the vocabulary lists. When he or she uses the /s/ on words, tick and date on the checklist.

Possession

The use of /s/ on the end of a word to indicate possession is also learned early. Here again, children with Down syndrome may clearly demonstrate comprehension of the possessive form but not be able to actually sound the /s/ on a word when speaking. They may use possessive pronouns such as 'mine' before using /s/ on words.

In your observation diary, keep a note of the way in which your child indicates 'possession' and the words that he or she is using. You will also be marking some of them on the vocabulary lists. When he or she uses the /s/ on words, tick and date on the checklist.

Function words

Prepositions

Some of the first grammatical words children master are prepositions, such as *"on"*, *"in"*, *"under"*. Games to teach the meanings of these are not difficult to plan. More difficult pronouns, such as beside, above, below, may not be understood by children of school age. These can be used in sentences and acted out by children in games.

In your observation diary, keep a note of the way in which your child indicates 'place' and the prepositions that he or she is using. You will also be marking them on the vocabulary lists.

Pronouns

Pronouns are a little tricky to demonstrate, especially "I", "you", and "me". Games played in front of a mirror can help, pointing to yourself while modelling "I" and helping your child to do the same. Children usually refer to themselves using their own name or "me" before using "I". The use of 'carrier' phrases, such as "I like..." or "I see...", and their use in home-made books with photos of your child can help.

In your observation diary, keep a note of the way in which your child indicates 'person' and the pronouns that he or she is using. You will also be marking them on the vocabulary lists.

Articles

The use of the articles "the" and "a", and others such as "some", takes a while to develop. These words, and the auxiliary verbs such as "is" and "are", may be difficult because they add very little to the meaning of the sentence. They are also not stressed in normal talk and therefore may be difficult to hear and to process. In our experience, children with Down syndrome do not easily learn to use them in their language and they will be helped by reading them in sentences.

In your observation diary, keep a note of the way in which your child is talking and note down any use of articles. You will also be marking them on the vocabulary lists. When you have heard the use of "a" and "the" consistently, tick and date the checklist.

Tenses

There are many tenses in the language, but we have simplified them to present, future and past tenses. To use many tenses properly, an auxiliary or 'helping' verb is used, for example, "He is going", "They will be going", "He has been", "They are running". It takes most children with Down syndrome a number of years to master the use of auxiliaries and some individuals never learn to use them. However, most children do learn to use present, present progressive and simple past and future tenses to convey these meanings appropriately.

Children use the present tense of verbs first, for example "push", "jump", "sleep", "run", and this is the way most of the verbs appear in the vocabulary checklists.

Present progressive tense

The next tense children learn is the present progressive 'ing' form, for example, "pushing", "jumping", "sleeping", "running". To use this form correctly in sentences they need to use auxiliary verbs - for example, "I am pushing", "he is jumping", "they are sleeping", "we are running". You will note that the auxiliaries change with the pronouns ("I am", "he is", "she is", "Mummy is") and with singular or plural agents ("He is", "they are"). However children will use the 'ing' form of the verb on its own before they begin to use the auxiliaries.

When you hear your child using 'ing' on verbs, tick and date the checklist.

Past tenses

The past tense of verbs comes in two forms, regular and irregular. The regular form is the 'ed' form, for example, jumped and pushed. The irregular forms are all different and have to be learned individually, for example, slept and ran. A number of irregular past tense forms are often learned by children before they use the 'ed' form.

Irregular verb list - for verbs on the vocabulary checklists

Verbs from Vocabulary Checklist I

bought	☐ _/_/_	put	☐ _/_/_		
came	☐ _/_/_	ran	☐ _/_/_		
cut	☐ _/_/_	sat	☐ _/_/_		
drank	☐ _/_/_	saw	☐ _/_/_		
ate	☐ _/_/_	threw	☐ _/_/_		
fell	☐ _/_/_	took	☐ _/_/_		
gave	☐ _/_/_	were	☐ _/_/_		
had	☐ _/_/_	went	☐ _/_/_		
made	☐ _/_/_				

Verbs from Vocabulary Checklist 2

bit	☐ ___ / ___ / ___	hid	☐ ___ / ___ / ___
blew	☐ ___ / ___ / ___	hit	☐ ___ / ___ / ___
broke	☐ ___ / ___ / ___	read	☐ ___ / ___ / ___
built	☐ ___ / ___ / ___	rode	☐ ___ / ___ / ___
drew	☐ ___ / ___ / ___	said	☐ ___ / ___ / ___
drove	☐ ___ / ___ / ___	sang	☐ ___ / ___ / ___
fed	☐ ___ / ___ / ___	stood	☐ ___ / ___ / ___
found	☐ ___ / ___ / ___	swam	☐ ___ / ___ / ___
got	☐ ___ / ___ / ___	swung	☐ ___ / ___ / ___

Verbs from Vocabulary Checklist 3

caught	☐ ___ / ___ / ___	shook	☐ ___ / ___ / ___
choose	☐ ___ / ___ / ___	slid	☐ ___ / ___ / ___
dug	☐ ___ / ___ / ___	stuck	☐ ___ / ___ / ___
felt	☐ ___ / ___ / ___	swept	☐ ___ / ___ / ___
flew	☐ ___ / ___ / ___	tore	☐ ___ / ___ / ___
heard	☐ ___ / ___ / ___	told	☐ ___ / ___ / ___
held	☐ ___ / ___ / ___	thought	☐ ___ / ___ / ___
lost	☐ ___ / ___ / ___	woke	☐ ___ / ___ / ___

Regular verbs

Use of the 'ed' ending

For typically developing children, there is a stage when they seem to realise that 'ed' on the end of a word creates a past tense and they 'over use' it - saying buyed, or goed, for example. In our experience, children with Down syndrome rarely do this but we would be interested to know if you hear your child doing this.

In your observation diary, keep a note of the way in which your child indicates past events and his or her use of the 'ed' ending. In order to use the past tense and to help your child understand, a wall chart for the week or the month can be a great help. Mark significant events on the chart, then you can look at it with you child and say *"Yesterday, we went to the park"*, or *"Last week, we rowed a boat on the pond at the park"*.

There are other past tense constructions such as *"we have been"*, *"he has jumped"*, *"he might have jumped before"*. We suggest that you leave these to develop with literacy. If at the stage your child is learning to read, you help him or her to keep a simple diary, you will find that you begin to use these constructions.

Children with Down syndrome will understand the language more quickly if the examples used refer to their own activities and actions, rather than to characters in a book - hence the value of keeping a diary.

In your observation diary, keep a note of the way in which your child talks about past events. Think of ways to expand his or her own sentences to fully grammatical ones to then practice.

Future tenses

The future tense comes next but again needs the use of auxiliaries and the verb 'go', for example *"We are going to Grandma's house"*, *"Daddy is going to work on Monday"*, *"You are going to school tomorrow"*, *"He is going to school tomorrow"*.

The wall planner for the week or the month will help you to use future tenses and to encourage your child to do so. Mark the future events in the next week and talk to your child about them. As your child gets older, you can extend the planner to cover the year - and teach days of the week, seasons, months, weather - time words, tomorrow, today - and time concepts - next week, last month - all with reference to events on the wall planner that your child takes part in.

In your observation diary, keep a note of the way in which your child talks about future events. Think of ways to expand his or her own sentences to fully grammatical ones to then practice.

More advanced structures

There is a lack of research into the emergence of more complex structures in children's language and even less research on effective ways to teach children to use them. However, there is evidence to indicate that both modelling by expanding your child's utterance to the correct sentence and getting your child to imitate by copying you or by reading, are both important strategies.

The examples included here are those that may be needed early in school, such as comparatives, and those that occur in assessments of children's grammar. More research is needed on the development of grammar in the spoken language of children with Down syndrome and we suggest that you continue to use your observation diary to note down the sentences your child is using as a basis for deciding how to extend them.

Comparatives

Once children have some understanding of words such as big and small, they move on to understanding that size can be relative:

> *"Big, bigger, biggest"*

> *"Small, smaller, smallest"*

> *"Daddy is taller than Mummy"*

> *"Jenny is taller than Bob but Mummy is taller than Jenny"*

In this example, Daddy is the tallest and Bob is the smallest. Many children with Down syndrome will be in junior school or older before they really understand comparatives. We have used the example of height because it is easy to choose real life examples from family or school friends to teach it.

More complex sentences

There are many more complex sentence constructions such as embedded clauses, passives and the use of 'but not' for example. You may not feel that your child needs to be able to use these but they are included to aid further development for children who are making good progress and are reading and writing at junior school level or above (8 years and older). Many complex sentence forms will be used in children's reading books at this level and children's ability to understand what they read will be undermined if their grammatical knowledge is too limited.

Embedded clauses

"The dog chasing the cat is black" and *"The boy who is hungry is getting his dinner"* are examples of sentences containing embedded clauses.

A child who can understand, *"The dog is chasing the cat"* and *"The dog is black"* as two separate sentences, may not understand the compound sentence. Picture material can be used to help children to understand these expressions. For children with Down syndrome, reading them in order to support learning to understand them will help, as their limited verbal short term memory skills may make these sentences difficult to listen to and process.

Passive sentences

"Sally is being teased by her brother", *"The cat is being chased by the dog"* are examples of passive sentences.

"The cat is being chased by the dog" is the passive form of *"the dog is chasing the cat"*. Many typically developing children do not master passives until they are in school and reading from books. If you wish to teach this construction to older children, again use their everyday experiences to make teaching materials. They can act out - for example, *"Jenny is brushing Annie's hair"* to *"Annie's hair is being brushed by Jenny"* - and then write the two examples down under a picture of the action: *"Billy is cleaning the car"* or *"the car is being cleaned by Billy"*.

X but not Y sentences

"It is windy but not raining", *"Billy has fallen over but he is not crying"* This type of sentence can be taught with actions and simple picture materials.

These are just some examples of complex sentences that we all use. However, we would remind you that if you listen to what your child wants to talk about and then expand their utterances into correct sentences, you will teach them all the useful grammar that they need. Always try to teach using examples that are relevant to your child and can be used by them often when they want to talk.

Notes

Notes

DOWN SYNDROME
resources
and activities
ra

Down Syndrome Resources and Activities is a range of teaching materials, assessment and recording resources, designed for use with children with Down syndrome and children with similar learning difficulties.

Suitable for use at home and school, by parents, teachers, and speech and language therapists, these materials have been designed and evaluated by expert researchers and practitioners.

For the latest information on the series, see the *Down Syndrome Resources and Activities* web site at http://www.downsed.org/dsra/ or contact The Down Syndrome Educational Trust.

Series Editors

Sue Buckley is a psychologist, Emeritus Professor of Developmental Disability in the Psychology Department at the University of Portsmouth, UK and Director of Research and Training at The Down Syndrome Educational Trust. Sue has been actively involved in researching the developmental and educational needs of children with Down syndrome since 1980. She is an internationally recognised authority and has published widely for parents, professionals and researchers. One of Sue's three children, Roberta, is a young adult with Down syndrome.

Gillian Bird is a psychologist and Director of Consultancy and Education at The Down Syndrome Educational Trust. Gillian has been working with children with Down syndrome, from birth to teenage years, and their families since 1983. She has developed and supported the successful inclusion of children with Down syndrome in mainstream education since 1988. Gillian has also developed early intervention programmes and been active in research, publishing and training with colleagues.

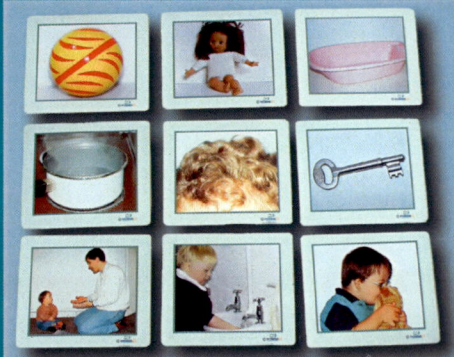

Also available from The Down Syndrome Educational Trust -

Down Syndrome Issues and Information is a unique range of publications that provide comprehensive information and practical advice about the range of developmental, health and social issues related to Down syndrome in a concise and accessible format.

DOWN SYNDROME issues and information *ii*

Written by expert researchers and practitioners, each section addresses a specific topic with a clear overview, practical guidelines and advice, and references for supporting material and additional resources.

Designed to meet the needs of parents, teachers, speech and language therapists, psychologists, and healthcare professionals, all advice and information is based on the latest scientific knowledge and wide, practical experience.

For further information, see the *Down Syndrome Issues and Information* web site at http://www.downsed.org/dsii/ or contact The Down Syndrome Educational Trust.

the DOWN SYNDROME educational trust

A registered charity, number 1062823

ISBN 978-1-903806-37-1

9 781903 806371 >